FUN FACTS ABOUT SPACE

Easy Read Astronomy Book for Kids
Children's Astronomy & Space Books

BABY PROFESSOR
EDUCATION KIDS

Speedy Publishing LLC

40 E. Main St. #1156

Newark, DE 19711

www.speedypublishing.com

Copyright 2017

In this book, we're going to talk about some fun facts about outer space. So, let's get right to it!

WHAT IS OUTER SPACE?

If you're living on Earth, as soon as you travel about 60 miles or about 100 kilometers off the planet's surface, the atmosphere disappears. When there's no air left, the typical blue color that we see in the sky isn't there any more. Molecules of oxygen are what give the sky its distinctive color. Beyond the blue, there is blackness and now you've reached the edge of outer space.

Lunar Lander

When we fly an airplane, there is friction due to the atmosphere, but in the vacuum of space there isn't any "drag" on a satellite or spacecraft that's traveling. That's why the Apollo program's lunar lander didn't have to have a streamlined shape. Instead it's very odd-shaped and looks like a giant spider. Because it was going to a location with no atmosphere, namely the moon, it didn't have to be designed for the friction of breaking through air.

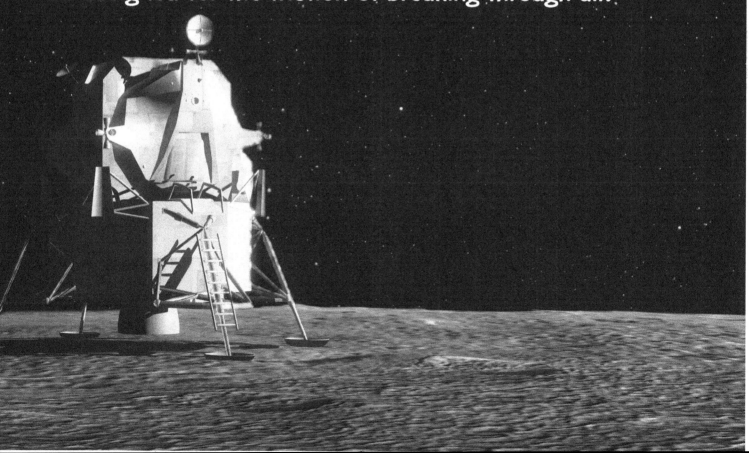

ARE THERE SOUNDS IN OUTER SPACE?

Sound travels in waves and it needs a medium to travel in, such as air or water. This means that in outer space there isn't any sound. The molecules of matter that are out in space aren't close enough to carry sound. In areas where there are no celestial bodies, space is essentially a vacuum, which simply means it doesn't have any matter.

If you were on another planet and there was enough of an atmosphere, it would carry sounds just like on Earth. You may wonder how astronauts talk to each other when they are out in space since sound doesn't carry. Astronauts communicate using radio waves, which is a type of electromagnetic radiation.

Our universe is enormous with vast sections of empty space and some "neighborhoods" that are crowded with stars, planets, galaxies, and other types of matter.

HOW BIG IS SPACE?

Scientists don't know how big space is. The distances in space are so vast that we measure them using a unit called a "light-year." One light-year is the distance that light travels in a year of time. Light travels 186,282 miles every second! It's hard to understand how light can travel this fast. In a year's time, light would travel 5.8 trillion miles.

The light that we can see using telescopes makes it possible for us to see galaxies that are almost as distant in time as the Big Bang. Scientists believe that our universe is about 13.7 billion years old. That means that the size of our universe, at least what we can see of it, as measured in light-years is 13.7 billion. However, just because this is as far as we can measure doesn't mean that space doesn't continue. Space could be a lot bigger if other universes exist.

WHAT TYPE OF RADIATION IS THERE IN SPACE?

Outer space appears to be empty, but our eyes aren't the only judge of what's out there. Sometimes our scientific instruments can detect things that we can't see. Astronomers know that in between celestial bodies, there are bits of matter in the form of dust and molecules of gas.

In addition to dust and gas, there are different types of radiation in space.

Aurora Borealis

SOLAR WIND

The sun emits plasma as well as particles in the form of solar "wind," which flies out toward the planets and causes the aurora borealis or Northern Lights at our poles.

COSMIC RAYS

Supernovas, which are huge exploding stars, emit these rays.

Supernova

Cosmic Ray

COSMIC MICROWAVE BACKGROUND

These microwaves are from the original Big Bang and are the very earliest form of radiation that our astronomical instruments can detect.

WHAT ARE DARK ENERGY AND DARK MATTER?

Scientists are still trying to figure out exactly what dark energy and dark matter are. Even though they can't be seen, they are known by the effects they have on other elements of the universe.

Dark Matter particles

Dark Energy makes up about 68.3% of the universe. It's responsible for the expansion of the universe, which has been accelerating for about 7 billion years.

Dark Matter makes up about 26.8% of the universe. It interacts with the other elements of the universe through its gravity. Astronomers can see that light is bending from the gravity of objects that are invisible. This effect is called "gravitational lensing" and is a clue that Dark Matter exists. Another clue is that stars are traveling in orbits around their galaxies faster than they would under normal conditions so it points to Dark Matter having an influence on gravity. If there is a large amount of matter that we can't see, then it influences the mass as well as the rate of rotation of a galaxy.

Normal Matter makes up 4.9% of the universe. This is the type of matter we can see like stars, planets, and other celestial objects.

BLACK HOLES

When stars die, they sometimes collapse in on themselves forming a massive black hole. The gravitational pull from a black hole is so strong that not even light can escape it, that's why it was named "black hole." Astronomers don't know what exists inside the black hole or what exactly happens when something gets pulled into it. Famous physicist Albert Einstein predicted that black holes were so powerful that they would cause ripples or waves in space and time.

Black Hole

Black Hole

Because space and time are connected, time accelerates or slows down if space is distorted by an intensely strong gravitational pull. In 2017, astronomers discovered evidence of the gravitational waves produced in space when two black holes interact or merge together. They hope to find out more about the properties of black holes by studying these cosmic events.

WHAT TYPES OF CELESTIAL BODIES ARE THERE IN THE UNIVERSE?

There are many types of objects out in space and astronomers are always researching to find out more about them.

Sun

STARS

Our sun is a star. A star is essentially a huge ball of different gases that emits radiation. Some stars are red supergiants. Some are white dwarfs that have been cooling down since they exploded in supernovas. These supernova explosions send out elements, such as iron, throughout the universe. They can also create very dense celestial bodies called neutron stars. Some neutron stars give out radiation in the form of pulses so they are a special category named pulsar stars.

PLANETS

In 2006, astronomers began to more clearly define how planets should be categorized. They determined that planets should have these characteristics:

They should orbit the sun.

They should be big enough to be sphere-like in shape.

They shouldn't have too much debris in their orbits.

Based on this new definition,
they said that instead of
being a planet, Pluto was a
dwarf planet. Astronomers
are still debating this point.

EXOPLANETS

Exoplanets or extrasolar planets are planets that are similar to the ones in our solar system except they revolve around different stars than our sun. The first such planet was discovered in 1992 and since then thousands more have been found. Sometimes, other star systems have planets that are in formation and those planets are named "protoplanets."

Asteroid Belt

ASTEROIDS

Asteroids are essentially enormous rocks that are not large enough to fit the classification of planets. Astronomers believe that they were leftovers from the formation of the solar system. Most of the asteroids are in a span of space between the planet Mars and the planet Jupiter. This area is called the asteroid belt. Because Earth has been struck by asteroids before with devastating consequences, NASA and other organizations have programs in place to look for potentially dangerous ones.

COMETS

Comets, which are nicknamed "dirty snowballs," are icy celestial bodies that come from the Oort Cloud. As the comet heads out from the Oort Cloud toward our sun, some of its surface ice starts to melt sending out a tail behind it. Ancient peoples used to think that comets signaled danger or doom, but astronomers eventually proved that they had periods when they would return and were regular events in the solar system.

Comets

Milky Way Galaxy

GALAXIES

Some of the largest structures in space are galaxies, which are huge groupings of stars. Our solar system is situated in the Milky Way galaxy. There are several different shapes of galaxies. Some are like ellipses and some are more spiral in shape. Sometimes there are clusters of galaxies that are grouped together by gravitational forces.

QUASARS

An enormous black hole is sometimes situated at a galaxy's center. Although black holes can't be seen, astronomers know they're located there because of their gravitational pull. If the black hole is pulling in a lot of matter, it gives off radiation and is called a quasar.

Quasar

SUMMARY

Outer space is made up of elements we can't see like dark energy, dark matter, and radiation, as well as normal matter that we can see, such as stars and planets. Astronomers can see that our known universe is at least 13.7 billion light years in size, but we don't know yet whether there's more space in our universe that we can't see or whether there are other universes in addition to our own.

Awesome! Now that you know about what's out in space, you can read more interesting information about our own solar system in Baby Professor books like What is the Solar System?

CPSIA information can be obtained
at www.ICGtesting.com
Printed in the USA
LVHW061710260420
654466LV00007B/925

9 781541 914827